DIVINE PROVIDENCE
Sr. Dale with Kim Bauman

Edited by Jenny M. Fuller

Divine Providence

Copyright © Kim Bauman 2024

All Rights Reserved

No part of this book may be reproduced in any form,
by photocopying or by any electronic or mechanical means,
including information storage or retrieval systems,
without permission in writing from both the copyright
owner and the publisher of this book.

Publish Date December 2024
ISBN: 9798346255604

Dedication

This book is dedicated to my dear friend Sr. Dale who has made my life better, the Sisters of Divine Providence who have given their lives to make the world a better place, and to the sisterhood of women, our chosen "sisters", our friends, who sustain us in times of need.

Special thanks to those making this book possible:
Daphne Hajovsky
Jenny Fuller
And all the sisters who welcomed me into their world briefly, cheerfully answering all my questions. Thank you for sharing your stories and pictures.

Divine Providence:
Traditional theism holds that God is the creator of heaven and earth, and that all that occurs in the universe takes place under *Divine Providence* — that is, under God's sovereign guidance and control. According to believers, God governs creation as a loving father, working all things for good. Moreover, it is said, God is an absolutely perfect being. He is, first of all, omniscient or all-knowing: he knows of all truths that they are true, and of all falsehoods that they are false, whether they pertain to past, present or future. And God's knowledge does not change. Nothing is learned or forgotten with him; what he knows, he knows from eternity and infallibly. Second, God is omnipotent or all-powerful: anything that is logically possible, he can do. Finally, God is perfectly good: in all circumstances he acts for the best, intending the best possible outcome.
(Stanford Encyclopedia of Philosophy 2022)

Divine Providence:
(Lat., providere, 'to foresee'). The belief that all things are ordered and regulated by God towards his purpose.
("Providence" in The Concise Oxford Dictionary of World Religions)

To be abandoned to Divine Providence:
is to place ourselves and our world in the hands of God whose love and power accomplish more than we can understand. It is our trusting response to God, who leads us to live in justice, peace, freedom and love.
(Congregation of Divine Providence -
https://www.cdptexas.org > our-spirituality)

Table of Contents

Foreword

"What is a Nun?"

1 – Divine Providence
My meeting Sr. Dale...

2 – In Her Own Words

3 - Life in Pictures

4 - Other Sisters

5 – Shared Letters, Cards, and Articles

"The Virtue of Poverty"
by
Sr. Elizabeth Dale Van Gossen

Foreword

In a world often marked by division and uncertainty, the story of Sister Dale stands as a radiant testament to the power of faith, love, and education. *Divine Providence* invites readers from all backgrounds—especially those of us outside the Catholic tradition—to reflect on our own spiritual journeys through the lens of Sister Dale's inspiring life.

As a dedicated teacher, Sister Dale made a remarkable impact on her students, no matter where she taught. Her classrooms were vibrant spaces of encouragement and discovery, where every student felt valued and inspired to reach their potential. Her unwavering commitment to education illuminated the path for many, demonstrating that knowledge and compassion can transform lives.

This work is a rich tapestry of joy and inspiration, reminding us of our universal quest for meaning and connection. As I explored Sister Dale's journey, I found myself reflecting on my own beliefs and values. Her dedication to love, understanding, and service resonates deeply, inviting all of us to consider how we can embody these ideals in our everyday lives. *Divine Providence* not only celebrates Sister Dale's extraordinary legacy as a teacher and mentor but also encourages each of us to explore and enrich our own faith journeys. May her story inspire you as it has inspired me and so many.

Jenny M. Fuller

"What is a Nun?"

My Entrance into
the Novitiate,

Investiture Day
June 21, 1956

Your loving and
grateful daughter,
Dale

What Is A Nun

Nuns come in assorted sizes, weights, and wimples. They are found everywhere... swathed in, seated in back of, kneeling on, speeding down, prespiring over, shoping for, patroling along, worried about, or laughing at.

Little children idolize them, priest try them, non-Catholics gawk at them, and St. Joseph looks after them.

A nun has the neatness of a pin, the trust of a child, the daring of a paratrooper, the perseverance of a bill collector, the energy of a vest-pocket atomic bomb, the authority of an encyclopedia, and the versatility of a trouble-shooter.

She loves our Blessed Mother; likes a good meditation book, ice-cream, Friday afternoons, a letter from home, and Nun's Day. She isn't too keen on summer school, long sermons, correcting homework, or getting up early.

Nobody is so quick to praise, so slow to censure. Nobody else can give you a licking and cry while doing it (except my Mom). Nobody can skip rope or tell stories or write on the blackboard as well.

A nun is a wonderful creature. You can dirty up her classroom, but her devotion remains unsullied. You can sass her back, but her prayers for you are redoubled.

You can tax her patience, but never deny her influence for good. A nun is this and more, for she is God's Sweetheart, and it is no wonder He loves her!

"The Lord saw that the time had come for me to be loved. He made a covenant with me and I became His; He spread His garment over me, He washed me with the purfumes of His grace. He feed me with the finest flour, with honey and oil in abundance. Then I became beautiful in His eyes and He made me a powerful queen."

"You have not chosen Me, but I have chosen you."

Providence of God I resign myself to Thee this day; as Thou desirest so shall I live and die for Thee.

Chapter 1

Divine Providence
My meeting Sr. Dale...

Elizabeth Dale Van Gossen was born in Alexandria, LA to Irma Dale Greene and Ernest F. Van Gossen. There were nine children, including two sets of twins.

I first met Sister Dale in the mid 80's. I feel it was Divine Providence that we met, as we became great friends, and she was a comfort to me throughout the rest of my life. I went to an interview for a teaching position in Ennis, Texas. She did not look like a nun. There was no habit. I was hoping for the flying nun, having watched that faithfully in my childhood. As an unexperienced teacher, I was more like Sally Field, getting into scrapes and Sr. Dale gently guiding me back to solid ground. Oh, I had so many great ideas that year. Each time I went to Sister Dale with an idea of something just wonderful we could do to enhance education, she welcomed me with a smile. Now, I realize, she had to be bracing herself for another pie in the sky suggestion!

We became friends, even though there was a twenty-year age difference, because I spent so much time in her office. We got to know one another. I had no children at that time and spent much time at school. She let me have the first EARTH DAY celebration for that school. I put on a terrible SNOOPY play at Christmas. The chili cook-off my class hosted resulted in us blowing out all the electricity in the school building. Who knew you could not plug in a dozen crock pots and electric skillets? At the time, I resented that everyone came to my classroom to see the cause of the outage. I mean really, couldn't it have been someone else? Perhaps a natural disaster or forgetting to pay the bill? Yet, it does symbolize the type of year Sr. Dale had to put up with in hiring me. I never felt anything but support from her. Never has or will my patience equal hers.

This week the Great State Fair of Texas is opening. The fair became a treasured tradition for my family. My husband and I took our daughter at least 20 times! Yet, the first time I rode the huge Ferris Wheel was with Sister Dale and two other nuns from the school. We went to the State Fair of Texas one evening after school. Sister Dale was driving. She exceeded the speed limit all the way there. I think it is the only time she has ever broken the law. I don't know what was scarier, her driving on the highway to Dallas or riding the tallest Ferris wheel in the United States. My only thought on both was that I would die in good company.

The only other surprise I've had from Sister Dale is her love of going to the casinos. In her defense, I think she sets a very low limit for gambling. The only time I ever heard her say she won a little more, she spent it taking her companions out to dinner on the way home! Even then, she ordered from the value menu.

When I sent used purses from friends to the convent, everyone was very grateful. I did it after I learned that the nuns kept one purse. I guess that really is all you need, but can you imagine? I change purses with the seasons! Not only did she feel guilty keeping an extra one, now she had two purses, all the designer purses went to the auction to raise money for the poor! It is no wonder few young people are choosing to become a nun. Not only are we a very worldly, selfish society, there are many other ways to serve the church today. Before Vatican II, only nuns could touch the altar cloths and do certain jobs for the priests and church. Now, many lay people do those jobs, are readers, and help the poor. Women also have many more choices for life. It is not, get married or be a nun. It is not, be a nurse or a teacher or stay home. Society has changed. Yet, the need for selfless people is never going to change. The contribution to the world and mankind is all the better for having the sisters. They are a dying breed, not just in profession, but in character.

I moved several times, and her hand painted cards became treasured keepsakes. Her suggestions for religious and social readings, movies, and political talks were thoughtful and interesting. Her point of view was of a highly educated Catholic and not based on just local interpretations. She grounded me, often.

I visited her more than once at the Mother House in San Antonio and every time was great fun. I always learn something from Sr. Dale. She is thoughtful and well read. She questions life and readings constantly, but she has never questioned her decision to be a nun. I asked her. Her unwavering dedication to her oath is only comparable to Queen Elizabeth of England. They are both a dying breed. I do not see that commitment in our youth, in myself, or in world leaders. She is unselfish and makes great sacrifices in her personal life for the greater good of mankind.

As I interviewed her friends, fellow sisters, and others, they all said the same thing. She is kind, she is giving, she is humble. Not one person even hinted at anything else. Her character alone is remarkable, even without her record of a life of service.

When she was in High School, she ran with a crowd of seven who were called the "gophers" and did normal High School activities. Except none of them had any "dirt" to tell on Sr. Dale! They honestly had good, clean fun. They played baseball in the farm fields, went to school dances, swam, and enjoyed the movies. Her best friend in High School, Leola, went to the convent after graduating, in August but left by Christmas. She just didn't have the vocation. They remained good friends.

Her story is that of what the church always says of us. We are saints in the making. She is well on her way. It has been a great comfort to me and my daughter that she and her congregation pray daily, for years, for the healing of my daughter who has a chronic illness. The name of her congregation, The Sisters of Divine Providence is appropriate and endearing. It is fitting. I love the name. The story of their being in Texas is amazing. These small, poor nuns saved pennies until they were able to build the magnificent, beautiful cathedral in San Antonio. Their founder, Father Moye, is celebrated every October at a festival at the retreat center in Castroville. The celebration is a community event. Father John Martin Moye (1730-1793) was a French Catholic priest who founded the Sisters of Divine Providence, a Roman Catholic religious order of women, in 1762. He was a parish priest in Lorraine, France and was troubled by the lack of education in the area, especially for women. Moye sent young women into the rural villages to teach children. The women believed in the Abandonment to Divine Providence. They not only taught and educated in the rural area, but also spread this faith. The villagers called the women Sisters of Divine Providence. The Congregation of Divine Providence (CDP) took its final form in 1852. Father Moye was beatified by the Catholic Church in 1954. Moye died of typhus during the French Revolution in 1793. In 1866, two Sisters from Lorraine, France, traveled to the new diocese of Texas to establish schools. The Sisters began 24 Texas Catholic schools by 1886 and a branch of the Congregation of Divine Providence in Texas. All they had was their extreme trust in the Divine Providence of God.

Sr. Dale
March 2024

Chapter 2

In Her Own Words

The content in this chapter is a compilation of the stories and messages sent to Kim Bauman over the years by Sr. Dale.

One of my earliest memories is visiting my Grandma and Grandpa Van Gossen on Sundays and making necklaces out of Four O'clock blossoms. In the summertime, I would spend a week with Grandpa and Grandma Van Gossen on the farm and with Grannie and Papa Greene on their farm down passed Bunkie. On one occasion an old rooster spurred me just above my lip. I don't remember this, but I still have the scar and was told what happened. That old rooster ended up in the cooking pot soon after.

As a little girl I often went to Mass and Holy Week services (and the movies!) with my Aunt Jennie at the Cathedral downtown. (Aunt Jennie lived with us for a while when we lived in town.)

We had been living in town (Alexandria, LA), but in 1945 we moved to the country, Daddy having bought Grandpa's farm after he died. That was also the year my oldest sister went to the convent.

After we moved to the country when I was in 3rd grade, we went to 5:30 Mass at St. Rita Church, because Daddy wanted to go fishing or hunting. After I got my driver's license, we went so we could go swimming at Valentine Creek. The water was freezing cold! We used to go every Sunday and played softball every Saturday afternoon with the neighbors. St. Rita was a little white painted church, much like St. Augustine at the Isle. I made my Confirmation there, and Aunt Jennie was my sponsor. There is now a new St. Rita out on Bayou Rapides Road.

In grade school at Providence Academy there was a chapel. On First Fridays there was adoration, and I always liked to go make a visit. When I was in the 4th and 5th grade, I would help Sister dust and clean chapel.

When I was in the sixth grade I made my Confirmation. I got a little prayer book, and later started to pray with it often. I think that was the beginning of my private prayer practice.

That was the only time I had long hair. Aunt Jennie would give us home permanents. Before that Daddy always cut our hair like little Dutch girls... short and straight with bangs.

One time I went home with a friend from the school bus. The table was set out with all kinds of food. I said that we-didn't eat supper that early, and they replied back that it wasn't supper, just a snack! They were hard working farmer kids, so I guess they needed it. I was just a city girl living in the county, but I did chop and pick cotton for spending money.

In high school we had uniforms and road the school bus home. In high school we liked riding the school bus because the boys from Menard were also on the bus.

Once someone hit me on my seat. I thought it was Tiny B. who was my younger brother's age. I liked him and his older brother. They played ball with us on Sunday afternoons. I slapped him in the face! Come to find out it wasn't him, but Albert Mathews, one of the Mathews boys that ran around with my brothers. Albert, Richard, and Dump, as they were called, with Don, Dan, and Tilden, my brothers. Once they came to Mrs. Mathews yelling that Richard had been shot, scaring the life out of her. He had been shot with a bee'-bee gun! My Dad said what one didn't think of the other did. They were playing cops and robbers one time and had my youngest brother with a rope around his neck standing on a can. My cousin kicked it out from under him and he nearly choked to death!

We got into trouble one time throwing Cyprus balls at each other. The pastor came out and fussed at us.
After my sister Pat taught me how to drive ... during that process I turned in at our place and took the gate with me. Thought my Dad would be angry, but he just laughed.

I got my license, and after that took my younger brothers and sister and neighbors to ball games and to the drive-in. In the summer we would go to Valentine Creek to swim and have fun.

My love life ... if you want to call it that, started when my sister Pat was dating her future husband. Buddy Mathews was his cousin and went along with them. and I was invited. Eventually just Buddy and I went to the movies. I really didn't want to go with him, but didn't say anything. He gave me a Sweetheart Valentine. I wanted to tell him I wasn't his sweetheart! He once said he could just eat me up, but all we ever did was hold hands. He was then gone in the Army.

I had my driver's license and began taking my brothers and the neighbors to ball games and movies at the drive-in. Buddy heard about it and wrote me a letter telling me I was robbing the cradle because Aubrey was a year younger than me and that if I came back from the convent there would be hell to pay. I wrote back saying he was robbing the cradle since I was 4 years younger than him. And that if I came back any hell to pay would not be because of him.

Another boy from the school bus went out with me to a Saddie Hawkins dance. He asked if he could kiss me, and I said no. He should just have done it!

The other boy I really liked was Aubrey. He tried kissing me once at the drive-in, (with all the others in the car with us!) but I wouldn't let him. He wanted to know why, and I said because it couldn't go anywhere since I was going to the convent. When we were at ball games, he would put his jacket in front of me and we would hold hands up in the sleeves. After I went to the convent, he wrote to me telling me he was still waiting for his best girl! Of course, I never saw the letters, but Sister Ann Joseph told me to tell Lulu (a friend who knew us both) to tell him to stop writing that I was God's best girl now.

My group of close friends (we called ourselves "The Gophers") would go to movies and swimming and sometimes sneak into the drive-in by going in the exit I don't know if it was on purpose or an accident, but they didn't take the speaker off, and my Dad found it in the back of the car the next day! He told me to tell my friends they shouldn't leave the evidence behind and to take it back to the theater. Mary Aza, the friend I visited, was one of the "Gophers". We spent graduation night at a house her parents owned out in the country. They gave me a 7up with some liquor in it thinking I had never had any before, but my Dad used to give me Coke and Whiskey once and awhile when he would have one. She's also one of us that sneaked into the drive-in at the exit. Went to Junior Senior Prom with her brother. He made me so mad, because he never danced with me.

Our group used to go swimming out at Castor Plunge, a freezing cold pool fed by streams. Which reminds me of Valentine Creek, another freezing creek where I took my brothers, Mathews, and Bristers swimming most Sundays in the summer. Had a crush on Aubrey Brister. Also took them to the drive-in. A.B. was in the back, but he had his arms around me and brushed his thumb across my lips.
And to think I'm going on 86 and never been kissed!

Think I told you I chopped and picked cotton to earn spending money. Told Sonny Mathew I didn't know how to dance, and he said all you have to do is back up and push. He's the one who asked me if he could kiss me, and I said no. I asked him to a Saddie Hawkins dance, and A.B. and Kitty (his future wife) rode with us.

I was President of the Sodality and so got to crown the Blessed Mother in May of my senior year.

I graduated in May of 1954 and went to the convent. Had a great send off at the railway station. My best friend went also, but she didn't stay. Many years later her daughter asked me to send her any pictures I had of her mother, and I did. She in turn sent me a picture of her parents and their 4 children.

There were 14 of us when we entered the novitiate in 1956. Two left and we were 12 for several years.

My first mission was in Bunkie, LA teaching first grade. The story goes that the Major's little girl saw a monkey and couldn't say it right and called it a Bunkie, and that's how the town got its name. We borrowed the neighbor's car to go get groceries every week. Had 54 first graders one year ... the largest class I ever had. One little boy was trying to climb out the window. We had a dog, a Collie. The Superior loved it that's why! Another sister and I put on a Christmas Pageant one year. We spent lots of time making the rocks for the cave. Had done the same in Enid. Even though I was only about 20 miles from Alex. in those days we couldn't go visit home. My family came to visit me a few times while I was there. A funny thing happened on the train there. The convent would pack a lunch of sandwiches for us, but when we opened the bag there was on a big ham bone inside!

Getting close to the end or rather the beginning, I was in Lafayette, LA in 1961-63. Taught 1st grade and will never forget I was there when Kennedy got shot. We never used to watch much TV, but we did then! It was also the first time I was in a community that had a car. They were all making noise one time, and someone said to keep quiet, they were distracting the driver, but I told them it didn't bother me. I was used to driving a bunch of kids around. They laughed at that.

We made our final vows in '63.

In 1964-65 I was in Enid, OK. The only time I was in that state. Taught 3rd grade. It was a large community of about 12 or so, don't remember exactly. I do remember the delicious dinner rolls we got from the cafeteria. We would slice them up and use them for toast.

From 1966-69 I was in my favorite mission of all time, Broussard, LA. Guess it was because for the first time I had a relationship with the kids outside of school. They were over at the convent all the time. We had a Ping-Pong table in an extra room on 1st floor, and they liked to come over to play with us. This is also where I met Yvetty Girouard. She used to come over to my classroom on Sat. when I was working in my room. We still keep in touch. She stopped by to visit me when I was in Alex. and she was there for a ball game. She also went to San Antonio with my Mom, my niece, and I when the World's Fair was going on. Had my first car accident taking her home to Broussard. Ran into the back of a stopped car when I was fooling around with the air-conditioning. It was while I was in Broussard that we changed habits. The kids teased me a lot. Oh, and once I got angry, and left the room slamming the door and the crucifix fell off the wall! There was a deep Oh from all of them.

In 1971, I was in Shreveport, LA for just one year. Taught 6th grade. Father Buddy Ceasar was the assistant priest there. He was one of the oamiens who put out some beautiful hymns. Used their tapes in my classroom and taught the kids to sing many of their songs. Buddy left the priest hood but is still giving retreats and was working at a retreat center in New Orleans but is now at Maryhill in Alex. He's giving a retreat here June 5-12 and I'm making it.

Pray for me as I will for you. (to Kim)

Before that I was in Houston for 2 years. Started out teaching 5th grade but then the sister teaching junior-high Math left, and I was moved up to 7th and 8th grade Math and Religion. This was my first experience with junior-high and I really liked it. Good thing because that's what I ended up doing for the next 20 years! Loved the kids and had fun with them. When I was in the hospital (hectorectomy)? (couldn't find the darn word I the dictionary!) three of the boys come to see me. My Dad died while I was stationed there, but ironically, I was in San Antonio for a meeting when he had his heart attack. Had to fly home for the funeral.

We stopped wearing the habit in 1970. Then came all the changes in the Church and some left including my older sister. That was hard for me; she had always been there for me, and I looked up to her.
Then our group was down to 9. Now in 2021 we are only three left.

In 1979 I was in San Antonio for 2 years and taught Math over at St. Martin Hall across the street from the convent. It was connected to the University at the time and is now closed. At that time, they were
trying out this new method where 6-8 were all in the same room, and you were supposed to teach one group while the others did their work. You can imagine how well that went over! I lived at the back of
the campus with several sisters, one of which was the President of the University, Sister Elizabeth Ann. The New Library is named after her. One of my Novitiate members, Sister Michelene was also there, and
we enjoyed walking in the evenings. Another liked to go swimming, and I enjoyed going with her.

I was stationed in Ennis in 1981-1991. Taught 5 years and was principal of the elementary for 5 years.

This is when I met you! (Kim)

That's where Sr. Annalee and I became good friends. I had known Sr. Janez since grade school, but we too, became good friends in Ennis. We did some fun things together, like going camping at Annalee's friends' cabin in the woods and visiting a water place in Fort Worth. While some of us went for a walk, Janez stayed to take a nap. She made a fire in the fireplace and didn't open the flue, and when we got back the room was full of smoke! We told her we saved her life! It was Janez and Annalee that convinced me

I could be principal of the elementary school when Annalee left ... or rather called home to be the Coordinator of the convent. The fact that she and

Janez were in San Antonio made it a little easier When I was asked to come here.

In 1982 celebrated my 25th Jubilee. Some of my family came from home and my brother Dan from Besley, TX. When I left Ennis, I went on sabbatical to St. Timothy's Priory in Dover, Massachusetts. Took classes on Scripture, Jesus and a drawing class. Never thought I could draw anything but found out I could! We went into Boston a couple of times to see the sights. My sister, Dorothy, and her friend came to visit, and the 3 of us went on a trip up to Maine. The coast was beautiful! Also visited one of our sisters in Flagstaff and we went to the Grand Canyon. I went on several tour trips with my sister, Pat, and on an Alaskan cruise with her and a good friend.

Later I learned to paint flower greeting cards and still do that today.

While in Ennis I took a painting class, as I was asked to take an older sister, so I took the class also.

I had a little prayer corner in my room. I also painted some oil scenes and gave them to my family. Kept one of flowers which I have in my room.

In 1992, I was missioned at the Isle for the first time... Iberville, LA, was known as the Isle. Loved it there. The convent was right across the road from beautiful Cane River. Taught 3rd and 5th grades full time in Cloutierville, a very small town about 7 miles away. In fact, it isn't much of a town...just the Catholic Church, public school, a grocery store, gas station, a few homes... and that was it. Lived with Sisters Tilly and Virginia Clare. Virginia Clare loved to invite people over for supper. Tilly and I didn't like it too much because it was on school nites and we were tired.

In 2005, I was in Houston for only one year and substituted at St. Ann's Catholic School. Lived with Bern Bezer and Deborah Fuchs in what is called the Heights area. I had been with my Mom for a number of years and after she died, I wanted to get back in community. Bern invited me to come to Houston. We loved to walk around the block in the evenings.

Bern had the habit of picking up trash along the way. She is my very tall friend that comes and watches Netflix movies with me now. She lives in one of the mobile homes out back and works as a Hospital Chaplin.

I was in Bryan, TX for only one year (2006-2007). Did substitute teaching in a Catholic school. Went there mainly, because Sr. Tiolinda (Tilly), was having trouble with her eyes and needed someone to drive. We watched a lot of TV. She's the one who got me hooked on Netflix! Sr. Tilly and I were good friends since we had been together in Ennis. We went on 2 or 3 of Sr. Virginia Clare's bus tours together. One on the East coast and one on the West coast and one that took us to Niagara Falls. We bought matching wrap around skirts, took a ride on Maid of the Mist which went in back of the Falls, and walked all around the beautiful, flower filled park.

Then back to the Isle for 5 years. This was my second time there. I was in charge of Providence Mission, a program started by Sr. Ida Marie Deville to help the poor in the area. I also did substitute teaching in Cloutierville and Natchitoches. Loved to go walking and picked up lots of pecans in the fall. Was there 5 years. Mass was at 8:00 so we didn't have to get up real early, unless I got a call to go in to substitute. We prayed on our own in the morning and together in the afternoon.

Then I went back to Alex. and was principal of St. Rita Catholic School for 5 years. Lived with my mother, who had had a stroke and could no longer live alone. A sitter was with her during the day while I was at work.

The family got together when my brother from CA came to visit. Those of us close by often got together at my sister Pat's at Christmas time. Now when I go home, I stay with my sister Jean. Her daughter lives right across the street.

And you and Mark had Emma! Have lots of her pictures from the proud parents.

My sister Dorothy who had been in the convent and left, got married when she was 71 to a wonderful man who was 81. They met at a square-dancing club and had 10 happy years together before he died.

My brother Dan had a big 65th birthday party. I was in Houston at the time, so a sister friend went with me. Dan is such a cutup, he kept us laughing. On Mom's 90th birthday we gave her a party, and Dan gave her 90 one-dollar bills! She laughed and laughed.

Made my 50th Jubilee while I was in Alex. Had a big celebration at the parish where I was principal.

After I celebrated my 50th Jubilee I went to Hawaii with my sister Dorothy and her friend Mary Ann. It was great I flew over a volcano on a little plane ride.

In 2011, Dorothy and I went out to CA to visit Johnny and his family In Riverside. He had 3 daughters by then and while we were there his first boy was born. Happy day!

Also in 2011, I was asked to come to San Antonio to our retirement center to be a Coordinator. After one year I asked to be an assistant to the Coordinators instead. I have been at that job now for 11 years. My main work is in providing for the incontinent needs of the sisters ... ordering, unpacking and distributing.

I also take care of providing cards and gifts each month for those celebrating birthdays, fix flower bouquets for the sisters in McCullough Hall.

Other than that, I am in the office for whatever is needed ... sewing on name tags or taking them off, cleaning out a sister's room when she dies, typing up the budgets and in what denominations the sister wants ... pay the hairdresser who comes to do the sisters' hair in McCullough Hall, help people with the copy machine etc.

I also take Communion to the sisters every Tues. and Wed. and on the 1st, 3rd, and 5th Sunday.

Sometimes I go with a sister to the hospital or doctor.

Once a month I am on duty over the weekend to take care of whatever may come up... Then I am off on Thurs. and Friday when I paint my cards or read or go shopping.

Don't get up until 7:00! What a treat that is after all the years of getting up at 5:00!

Breakfast is at 7:30. Then I go back upstairs and pray until around 9:00 when I go to the office.

We eat at noon. Mass is every afternoon at 4:40 except when we have birthday celebrations or community meetings on the 2nd and 4th Wednesdays. Evening meal is at 5:00 after Mass.

In evenings I watch the news and other TV programs or read. Usually go to bed at 10:30.

On Sunday afternoons, my friends and I play Rummy Cube and enjoy it a lot.

That's how my life here goes.

My 60th Anniversary was celebrated here in San Antonio, and some of my family were here. It was a hard mission to come to San Antonio, because I knew I'd be here for the rest of my life, be living in a big institutional building, and not have parish life anymore, but many blessings have come to me here. I became a good friend with some sisters here and with others I had been with on mission.

God is good and life is great!

A picture drawn by Sr. Dale of her mother holding a grandchild.

Beyond Her Years

She's finally closed her eyes to this world she's known for almost 95 years.
Nine decades—a long and blessed life.
A mother to nine and Ernest's wife.
She grew up with six brothers just west of here.
Schooled and married and then took care
Of her daddy before his passing
Unto the Father's everlasting.

A quiet and gentle soul was she.
Southern born with the hospitality.
A catholic vision————she raised her bunch
Faithful to God and Papa's lunch
Of stewed potatoes and biscuits each day
Specially made and knuckled her way:
And rather than leftovers, she served instead
Biscuits with syrup————candy bread!

I heard tell of a story from her courtin' days
With ball dribblin' and hoop shootin' plays.
And another—when her twins were wee,
A small baby boy upon her knee
Needin' all a mother could give
Of love, nurturing that he might live.
So with her spirit she gave of herself
Unto her family, its wealth and its health.

A member of the Mothers' Club, she did her part.
Her boys to service-a prayer at heart.
Chores and kids kept her aprons manned,
Sometimes sitting for a pokino hand.
She lived at home 'til her daughters knew
A helping hand was needed to get her thru.
And when more was required, the Lexington was there
With those that could mend and tend her cares.

Until today————
With over nine decades of living done
She's outlived her husband and three sons
Called Nannie by more than seventy-four
She's gone on to live with the Lord.
She's finally closed her eyes to this world she's known for almost 95 years
And yet she'll always remain with us, a part of us
Lingering in the memories beyond her years---
Beyond our tears.

God bless Momma
Nannie
A Friend to so many.
We all loved her
And will miss her dearly.

Kim's Question Interview of Sr. Dale

Question 1:
What were the changes that happened in being a sister from when you entered to today's time? Clothing, jobs, money, rights, duties, living, etc.

The most obvious change was the habit...was glad for the change...more comfortable and easier to keep clean. But I loved the habit!
Before the late sixties we had no personal money; you had to ask the Superior for whatever you needed.
You were sent to any mission where the Superior thought you were needed without any input from you. Now you can ask to be sent to a particular mission of your choice and also have a decision as to where you will live. However, having the vow of obedience requires you to think about the common good and so what you feel God is calling you to do.

Question 2:
What in your faith/beliefs changed over the years after decades of study and prayer?
What doctrine/ faith belief is misunderstood by the masses? Were you surprised to realize a commonly held "rule" or belief was false?
What in your faith has helped you remain strong and a sister over the years?
What do you wish people understood about the Catholic faith? What do you think is the biggest misconception about the Catholic faith held by Catholics? Non-Catholics?

You ask hard questions!

The way I view God has changed from thinking God is up "there" to knowing God is within me and present everywhere. I think lots of people think of God as a strict judge when God is a loving, forgiving, and merciful God. Thinking that someone is going to hell for eating meat on Friday, or that if you aren't Catholic you can't go to heaven; these are false beliefs. God's love and grace has helped me *(remain strong)* as well as the example of family, teachers, and other sisters...all is gift.
One of the biggest wrong ideas about Catholics by non-Catholics is that we worship statues and that nuns serve priests. My Baptist grandmother thought this! As for Catholics, I think some believe too much in rules instead of loving God and people.

Question 3:
What is your favorite thing and least favorite thing about being a sister?

The main reason I became a nun was I wanted to show God how grateful I was for all the gifts given to me. I always wanted to be a teacher and a sister. I loved all my years of teaching first grade through tenth. Now I am serving my elderly sisters here at the convent center.
My least favorite thing is growing old and not being physically able to do all the things I would like to do, or live where I would choose, but that is true of everyone, not just sisters!

Question 4:
What influence did your mother and father have on your religious life and how did they react when you told them you were going to be a nun?

They sent us to Catholic school and saw that we went to Mass every Sunday. When the school had the Fatima statue with a rosary inside, it was sent home to a family for a week, and we said the rosary as a family then. Other than that, we were not that religious. As a child I had a May altar to Our Lady, but this devotion came more from school than home. And as you know my great aunt and older sister were CDPs. My older sister Pat and I would go to Mass during Lent if it wasn't one at school. We would give up candy during Lent and save it all up for Easter!

Question 5:
As time progressed, many more jobs and choices became available to women. Was there any opportunity in later years you thought you wished you'd tried?

No, I didn't. I always wanted to be a teacher and enjoyed it all my years of doing it.

Question 6:
What is a major difference of women joining the order now compared to when you joined. Difference of women today and difference of procedure and differences of expectations.

The women who join now are older, have degrees, or have jobs. We even have 2 who were married and have adult children. When I entered almost all of us were teenagers. The formation people have to take into account the differences in age and experience of the women coming now and also their spiritual maturity.

Chapter 3

Life in Pictures

Baby Dale

Dale in 6th grade
Her confirmation

Pat & Dale

Tudy, Pat & Dale

Lulu, Dale & Tiny

Don, Tilden & Lulu

High School Years

(As seen on Cover) I was President of the Sodality and so got to crown the Blessed Mother in May of my senior year.
May 1954

The day Sr. Dale left for the Convent.

Dale & her nephew, Paul

Dorothy, Dale,
Her Mother & Dad

Dale & her Dad

Cecila, Rhea, Barbara,
Nina, Leala, Dale

Novitiate Group 1956-57

Novitiate Group after getting black veils in 1957

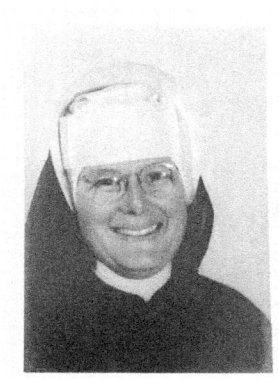

Prayer Corner in
Sr. Dale's room

Best friend in school and husband,
Leala & Jay Moore

One Christmas at Pat's

One of Sr. Dale's
Paintings

Adventures With Friends

Niagara Falls
7/19/1983
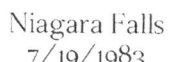

Alaskan Cruise

Dale & Pat
At the Field of Dreams
Movie Site in Iowa

After leaving Deadwood for
Mitchell Wall Drug

June 1994
Branson

"Crossing the Mississippi"

Christmas 1995

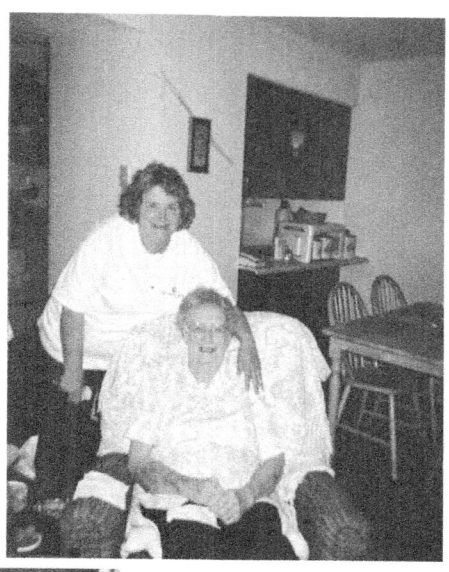

50th Jubilee
2007

Dorothy, Pat, Dale, Jean, her husband Jim, Dan

Pat, Dale, Jean, Dan

60th Jubilee
2017

60th Jubilee - 2017

"Growing up, I always wanted to be a teacher and a Sister, mostly because of the influence of my CDP (Congregation of Divine Providence) teachers and the fact that my great aunt and older sister were in the congregation. My life in ministry has been mainly in education, teaching first graders and on up to junior high and being principal. I have loved all my missions. The people I worked with, and the students. I feel grateful to God and most blessed for all the opportunities given me in my life as a Sister of Divine Providence."

Sr. Dale

2008 - Hawaii
Dale & Dorothy

2008 - Hawaii
Mary Ann & Dale

2004 - Pat's Family

Dale's brother Johnny, his wife and 2 sons, Jack & Aaron, Jack's wife and her mother and Jack's first daughter.

Sister Margaret Ann Verzwyvelt (left) and Sister Dale Van Gossen (3rd from left) fill boxes for the needy in Isle Brevelle, LA.

Don, Mom, Dorothy

Ronnie & Donnie

Dan's 65th B-day

Jeanette, Dan, Jean, Jim, Pat, Dale, Dorothy, Don

Jean, Dan, Dale

Don & Dorothy

Dorothy, Mom, Dale

Mom & the 8 of us!

Tilden, Dan, Don, John, Dorothy, Pat, Mom, Dale, Jean

BACK TO SCHOOL 2001

Meet the new principals

**St. Rita School
Alexandria, La.**

Sister Dale Van Gossen

Family: Sister Elizabeth Dale Van Gossen, a daughter of Ernest and Irma Van Gossen, is a Sister of Divine Providence whose Congregational Mother House is in San Antonio, Texas.
Hometown: Alexandria, LA
Education: She attended Providence Academy and Providence Central High School. Her BS and Masters degrees in Education were earned at Our Lady of the Lake University in San Antonio.
Teaching experience: Since 1957 Sister has taught in Catholic schools in Louisiana, Texas, and Oklahoma, first through tenth grades. She was principal of St. John School in Ennis, Texas, for five years. For the last nine years, she worked in the public school system, five years in Natchitoches Parish and four years in Rapides Parish. She is happy to be back in the Catholic school system.
Favorite saints: St. Theresa of the Child Jesus and St. Francis of Assisi.
Goals: To be an effective principal at St. Rita School and to make a difference in the lives of her teachers and students.
Hobbies: She loves to read and listen to music, as well as go to good movies.
Quote: "This is what Yahweh asks of you, only this: to act justly, to love tenderly, and to walk humbly with your God."

Dale

Mother Amata

After being Superior General, I was with her at OLP in Alex. where she started a Senior Citizen Org.

Chapter 4
Other Sisters

"The Congregation of Divine Providence was founded in Alsace-Lorraine, France in 1762. Since coming to the United States in 1866, the Sisters have served those in need in 150 cities, fourteen states and three foreign countries.

The Mission and Vision *(from the website cdptexas.org)*
We Sisters of Divine Providence are a community of women within the Catholic Church who dedicate our lives totally to furthering the mission of Jesus in the world. Rooted in profound confidence in God's providential love and care for all, we commit our lives, our ministries, and our resources to furthering the mission of Jesus. We envision a world in which, through Christ, God's way of justice, peace, freedom and love is manifest among all people and all creation.

Our Spirit, Our Four Fundamental Virtues
The fundamental virtues of our Providence Community—abandonment to Divine Providence, simplicity, poverty, charity—constitute our essential and unique spirit.

To be abandoned to Divine Providence is to place ourselves and our world in the hands of God whose love and power accomplish more than we can understand. It is our trusting response to God, who leads us to live in justice, peace, freedom and love.

To live in simplicity is to act always with a God-centered singleness of heart and purpose which enables us to come before God and our neighbor in sincerity of heart and mind. Our lifestyle is simple and unpretentious.

To live the virtue of poverty is to live without excessive goods and comforts, maintaining only what we need to carry out our mission. Freedom from dependence on possessions liberates us to do God's work.

To live by charity is to respond to the compassionate love of God by an outpouring of the words and deeds of mercy.

Act of Abandonment to Divine Providence

Providence of my God, I adore you in all your designs. I place my destiny in your hands, confiding to you all that I have, all that I am, and all that I am to become, my body and my soul, my health and reputation, my life, my death, and my eternal salvation. As I rely entirely upon you and expect all from your goodness, I will not give myself up to any useless anxiety. I confide to you the success of all my undertakings, and in all difficulties, I will have recourse to you as a never failing source of help. I know that you will either preserve me from the evils I dread, or turn them to my good and your glory. Peaceful and contented in all, I will allow your Providence to govern my life without worry or over eagerness.

Holy, wise, generous, and loving Providence! I thank you for the tender care you have taken of me up to this moment. I humbly and earnestly entreat you to continue the same for me; direct all that I do, guide me in your ways, govern me at every moment of my life, and bring me to the fullness of being that you have destined for me from all eternity. May I please you and give you glory forever. Amen.

Social Justice

With boundless confidence in God's Providence, we Sisters of Divine Providence embrace the mission of Jesus to be the incarnation of God's love in the world. Providence draws us to seek creative ways of opening our arms to the suffering and joy in all creation.

Believing in the power of Providence to bring all things to good, we commit ourselves

- to hear the cry of pain and anguish of the poor, immigrants, women, and Earth
- to be present as neighbor to all in need
- to act with courage and collaborate with others to heal what is broken and celebrate what is good in our world"

(CDP Chapter Statement 2017-2023)

Sr. Mary Ann Phillip

It was my absolute privilege to speak with Sr. Mary Ann who turned 100 years young in August 2024. She has known Sr. Dale and her family for many years. Of Sr. Dale she commented what so many others said, Sr. Dale is calm and gentle. She taught Sr. Dale's three brothers, Tilden, Dan, and Don in Alexandria, Louisiana.

She went to a Catholic High School 35 miles away, which was a great distance 80 years ago. She got her excellent work ethic from her family. Her mother was born in 1897 and her dad in 1895. They were pioneers who cleared the land. Her whole family picked cotton together in 1935 to buy a Ford V-8 car for 999.00. She thought "only stick in the muds" became nuns but changed her mind after prom. She wanted to do something with her life. In the summer after her Junior year, she visited the nuns in San Antonio. There were 750 sisters at that time. They were very happy. She decided to go into formation. It was a great disgrace to go home in those days. She needed to make a correct decision. There was a transplanted rose bush that never bloomed. She decided to pray a rosary every day and asked for guidance praying "Let the rose bush bloom" seeking a sign from God. When she had to make the final decision, three large white roses bloomed on it!

Her motto is to TRUST IN GOD. "Do what you can to make changes in what needs to be done. Everyone should vote for people who have correct values."

Sr. Mary Ann left. Sr. Bernadette right

4 siblings from the Phillip Family

Sr. Bernadette Phillip

Sister Bernadette is the biological sister of Sister Mary Ann Phillip. She celebrated 75 years of service in 2024. How wonderful it must be to have your own sister be with you on your faith journey.

It was in High School that Sister Bernadette felt the call to dedicate her life to God. She had many ministries including serving the poor in India. She also practiced Sahaj Samadhi meditation, and it transformed her life. Peace and human values are upmost in her heart and her choice of works.

She attended the World Conference on Spiritual Regeneration and Human values while in India. "My service in India was living simply, creating community, and experiencing the love that we are, and knowing that faith makes all things possible."

An Anonymous Sister

The stories of all the sisters are fascinating. Strong women on a mission, sometimes literally. All making personal sacrifices to fulfill a vow. All are doing their part to make the world a better place. All witnessing many changes in the church, especially after Vatican II. Yet there are not enough changes to bring them the recognition they deserve.

This Sister is the youngest of six children from Texas. Her mother and grandmother did not want her to become a nun. She became a sister in 1955. She looked to her older sister who was already a nun. Her 3rd sister became Sister Bernadette, when in the 1940's home visits were only every five years.

She was also influenced by an aunt. Her aunt dressed her as a nun when she had just finished first grade and ever since then, she knew she wanted to be a nun. At the time she was preparing to be a Novitiate by going to the convent on Sunday afternoons, there were 700 plus sisters there. She said the best thing about being a Sister is the community life. The hardest time she had was when she started teaching. Her preparation was not good. As a teacher myself now, nothing has changed on that account.

Her first assignment was double grades of first and second in Dallas. In 1968, the habits (clothing) changed. She was in the experimental group for lay clothes for six months. It was a black suit and a small veil. Now few sisters wear any veil and wear any modest clothing. She liked the new clothing as she could hear better. It was hard to hear with the head covered so tightly in the original layered head covering.

At her final vows, she had a wreath on her head, a wedding dress, and received a ring. There were 18 girls in her group.

Sr. Bern Bezner

Sister Bern Bezner was born in Lindsey, Texas on the Oklahoma border. It was a German Catholic community. The sisters taught in public schools. Her father had two sisters and three cousins who entered the Congregation of Divine Providence.

In High School, Sr. Bern fought the calling to join the convent. She really wanted to "get God off her back," so she decided to give it a try, and it was a challenge to not be sent home. She entered in 1965. Her mother and father were very proud of her. There were twelve in her novitiate, but only seven made their final vows. In 2027, she will make her 60th Jubilee. During the 1970s, many sisters left the convent. She had to choose to stay true to her vows every day. This strengthened her commitment. It was not easy and made her stronger. She did love the shared values and visions of the community.

She treasures her friendship with Sister Dale. She said Sr. Dale is a calming presence. She learns from Sister Dale who is an avid reader. The Quantum Theology by Ormushie was a particularly interesting study and conversation. It was about God not being static. Her admiration of Sr. Dale was evident and said she always dressed well and was classy. "She brings joy to each day."

The Congregation of Divine Providence of San Antonio welcomes your inquiries, support, reflections and other communication.

Congregation of Divine Providence
Our Lady of the Lake Convent
515 S.W. 24th Street
San Antonio, Texas 78207 – 4619
(210) 434-1866

Chapter 5

Shared Letters, Cards, and Articles

I've been trying to give them. And, thank you for the card. I am puzzled about why you used the word "envy." I know you can reach these kids! and I'm not just trying to be nice either. I have proof! Early in the year your students told me that you do "the Hokey Pokey!" That made me grin from ear to ear! Please don't forget to get your dancing shoes out. OK? Your students thought you were a pretty neat teacher for doing the hokey pokey.

                Love,
                Sue
              "Mrs. R♪"

May 28, 1994

Dear Sister,

I have received several presents these past two years at Cloutierville. I couldn't think of getting anything better than a day off or brunch for two. But, the most meaningful was from you and your class yesterday. I really must of had some self-control because the tears on the outside was nothing compared to what was going on in the inside! Every student was quiet during the introduction and they even looked like they were thinking about what they were about to sing! I guess what got me the most was they were giving back to me what I

SUE RODRIGUEZ

"The music teacher
when I was teaching
(lived at the Isle) in Clouterville.
I taught the kids a
song to sing for her.
"Sing a gentle love song
    To the earth.
Fill the air with music
    For her healing,
Then be still and you will
    Hear her love songs
Forever through the years."

Dearest Dale,
I wanted to do this for New Year and have it in your room. But a birthday is also the beginning of a new year and I'd like to share this with you. I can't begin to tell you how much I value your presence in community and I know I don't do a good job of letting you know this. You being yourself in a dimension of integrity which reflects itself in open-ness, candor, peace-making and good common sense. I admire your self-lessness and charity and your quiet, but very strong and direct way of getting things done. I also appreciate your simplicity in our community discussions. It's difficult to say here

all I'd like to, because words alone never adequately describe who a person is. I do admire and respect you, but above all I have learned to love you very dearly.
I pray for you a very happy day and I know you will enjoy the gifts of His Providence.
Very sincerely,
Liz Anne

Dale wrote at the bottom: Lived with Liz Anne 3 years when I taught at St. Martin Hall across the street from the convent. She was the president of the University at the time.

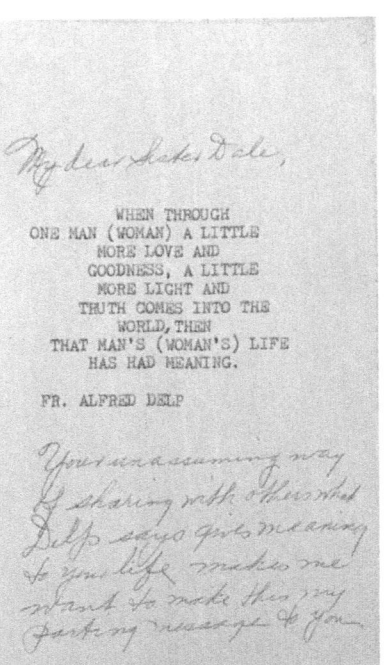

My dear Sister Dale,

Your unassuming way
of sharing with others what
Delp says gives meaning
to your life makes me
want to make this my
parting message to you.

You've done so many
beautiful things for others
especially sharing so deeply
what is truly part of you.

Shalom as you walk along the
way with Him.

Lovingly & prayerfully,
Sister Amata

Corpus Christi
June 13, 1982

"We hold out our hands. The (Eucharistic) minister says, 'Body of Christ.' 'Corpus Christi.' We answer: 'Amen.' 'Yes.' We say yes to peacemaking, through our own lives."
    Reflection by Pax Christi

 Thank <u>you</u>, Dale, for 25 years of saying "yes" to peacemaking through your vowed life as a CDP.
 Thank you especially for the many ways you have shared the "light of love; the wine of friendship; the bread of peace" with me.
 With my supportive prayer and love,

Marjet

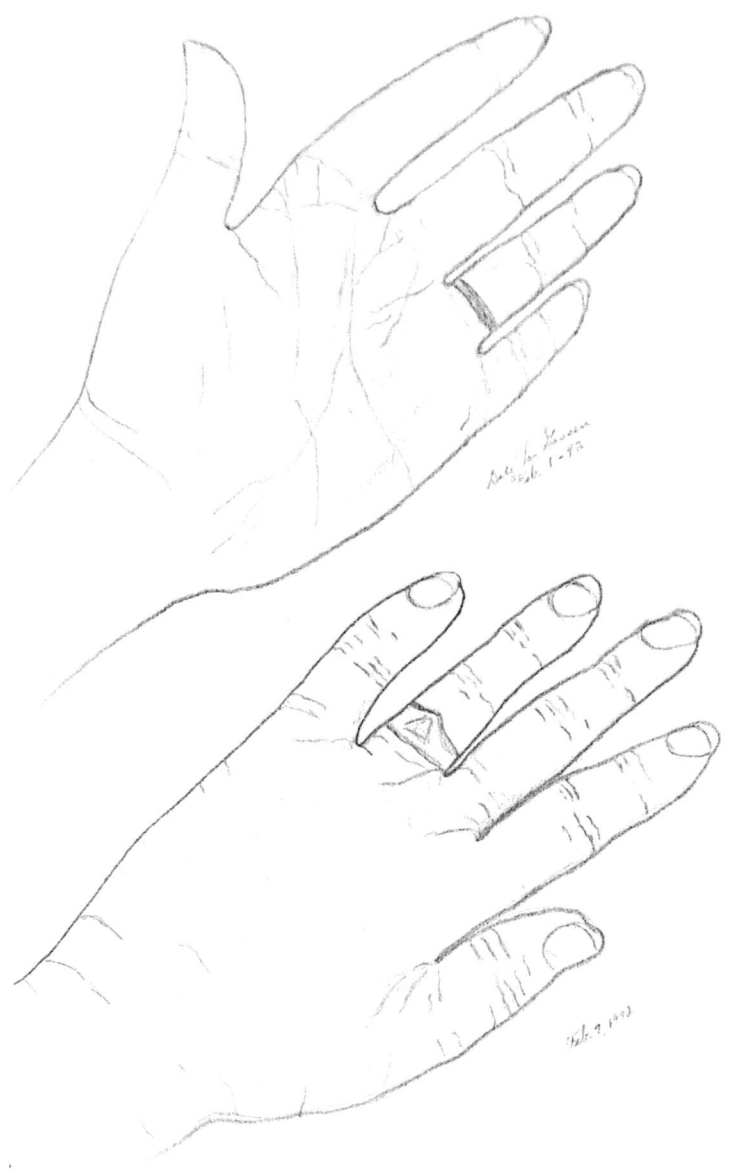

"The Virtue of Poverty"
by
Sr. Elizabeth Dale Van Gossen

When thinking about poverty I often feel guilty when I consider all that I have ... so <u>many</u> blessings and advantages. Someone once said we couldn't be poor because of our education and the opportunities we have.

Like most of you I've never really experienced real want or need. The fact is that such poverty is not a virtue...it is something we strive to overcome for ourselves and alleviate in other. What does the virtue mean then?

In my life it has come to mean being willing to share what I possess not only material things but myself... my time, my abilities, my love. It means trying to live more simply, and I think the virtue of poverty requires us to use God's gifts in a way that promotes equality and justice and certainly to give of our material possessions when possible. To try to lessen the consumerism in our society that uses so much of our world resources wastefully.

Before I go on would some of you like to share what you think the virtue of poverty means to you?

I've come to another more fundamental idea of the virtue of poverty. Whether you want to call it an attitude or a virtue ... either way I think it is the recognition and acceptance of our human condition ... to acknowledge that we are dependent upon God ..., that all is gift.

A priest giving an Advent mission in Bryan talked about materialism as putting things before people. He was saying there is nothing wrong with having nice things, of treating yourself to a well-deserved night out or a vacation. But that the sin of materialism today is the husband who comes home with his six packs, goes to the TV to watch his games all weekend and ignores his wife and family; or the teenagers glued to their iPods, video games, cell phones ... and never have any family interaction; or the woman so interested in her soap operas that her family and/or community suffer. What does that have to say about our spirit of poverty? Of using our gifts for others?

That same priest defined faith as a radical surrender of oneself. If we don't have that spirit of poverty where we recognize our dependence on God, it seems to me it would be very difficult to surrender one's self.

In a way all the virtues seem to need that fundamental insight that our basic human condition is one of poverty before God. Poverty is not just another virtue; it is a necessary ingredient in any authentic Christian attitude toward life.

One can be poor in many ways ... lack of talents, friends, position, recognition, emotional support, our inability to do something about the plight of our world and our society, _ the helplessness and powerlessness we feel about war, poverty, hunger, and disease in our world ... and yet trusting that God will bring about a solution in time.

Somewhere in one of his books, Ronald Rolheiser says we will always be wanting more for God has created us for the infinite. Like St. Augustine's famous saying: our hearts are made for you, oh God, and will be restless till they rest in You! Our present finiteness is part of our poverty.

The poor are those who let go of themselves and come to know that they can't rely on their own strength alone to reach salvation. They have to rely on God. The recognition and acceptance of that is to me part of practicing the virtue of poverty. Acceptance that's the hard part.

To be human is to be poor... to have nothing one might brag about before God.

Christ experienced the poverty of the human coindition more deeply than other persons possibly could. In his little book THE SPIRIT OF POVERTY, Father Johannes Metz wrote about Jesus temptations in the desert. And he, says they were assaults on Jesus' poverty.

His poverty of neediness.... wanting food.

His poverty of being.... just another human being, the common place, not using his power to be other than human.

His poverty of being unique and superior...the old saying "it's lonely at the top".

There is the poverty of the provisional nature as human beings ... we cannot rest in the security of the present... our life does not stand still; we must face the future and what is yet to be.

There is the poverty of finiteness; we live in a future of potentialities, yet every decision involves the sacrifice and surrender of a thousand possibilities.

There is the poverty involved in relationships; every genuine human encounter must be inspired by poverty of spirit... we must forget ourselves in order to let the other person approach us.

There is the poverty of death... in abandoning ourselves to poverty, we abandon ourselves to God ... who is the giver of all gifts.

When I was very young, I wondered how Adam and Eve thought they could be like God or why it was wrong that they wanted to be like God; Isn't that what we are supposed to be trying to be..... like God???

Now I think I know why. They wanted the power and control they thought God had to make things happen the way they wanted things to be. And I realize that very often that's what I want... to be in control, to have things the way I want them, to have the power to change things. The spirit of poverty then is for me to realize and accept the fact that I don't have the power... often even to change things in myself that I don't like. I am often helpless to bring about the good I would like to accomplish, powerless in the face of so much in our world and in my life. Accepting the reality of my human condition **requires** surrender and trust in a provident God ... that is the spirit of poverty.

To accept all that is... is what the spirit of poverty has come to mean in my life.

In one of St. Ignatius of Loyola letters he wrote:

'Poverty is none of that attachment which, like a band, binds the heart to earth and to earthly things and deprives us of that ease in rising and turning once more to God. It enables us to hear better in all things the voice... that is the inspiration... of the Holy Spirit by removing the obstructions which hinder it. It gives greater efficacy to our prayers in the sight of God because... God hears the cry of the poor. It speeds us on our way along the path of virtue like a traveler who has been relieved of all burdens. It frees us from that slavery common to so many of the world's great ones, in which everything obeys or serves money.'

Made in the USA
Coppell, TX
03 March 2026

73170430R00046